THE NORTHUMBERLAND
COLOURING BOOK

First published 2016

The History Press
The Mill, Brimscombe Port
Stroud, Gloucestershire, GL5 2QG
www.thehistorypress.co.uk

Reprinted 2017

Text © The History Press, 2016
Illustrations © Tom Kilby

British Library Cataloguing in Publication Data.
A catalogue record for this book is available from the British Library.

ISBN 978 0 7509 6797 6

Cover colouring by Lucy Hester.
Typesetting and origination by The History Press
Printed in Great Britain

THE NORTHUMBERLAND

COLOURING BOOK

PAST AND PRESENT

Take some time out of your busy life to relax and unwind with this feel-good colouring book designed for everyone who loves Northumberland.

Absorb yourself in the simple action of colouring in the scenes and settings from around the county of Northumberland, past and present. From iconic architecture to picturesque coastal vistas, you are sure to find some of your favourite locations waiting to be transformed with a splash of colour. Bring these scenes alive as you de-stress with this inspiring and calming colouring book.

There are no rules – choose any page and any choice of colouring pens or pencils you like to create your own unique, colourful and creative illustrations.

Northumberlandia ▶

Also from The History Press

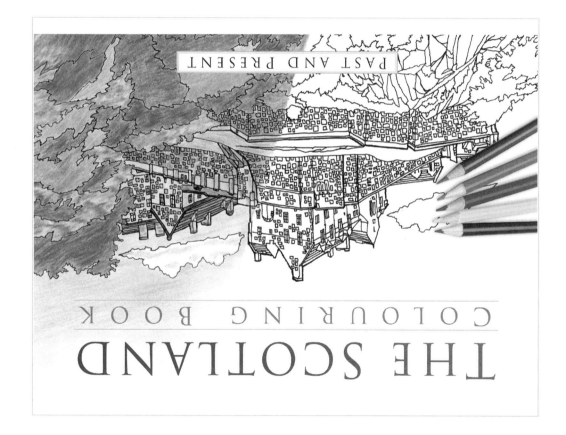

PAST AND PRESENT

THE SCOTLAND
COLOURING BOOK

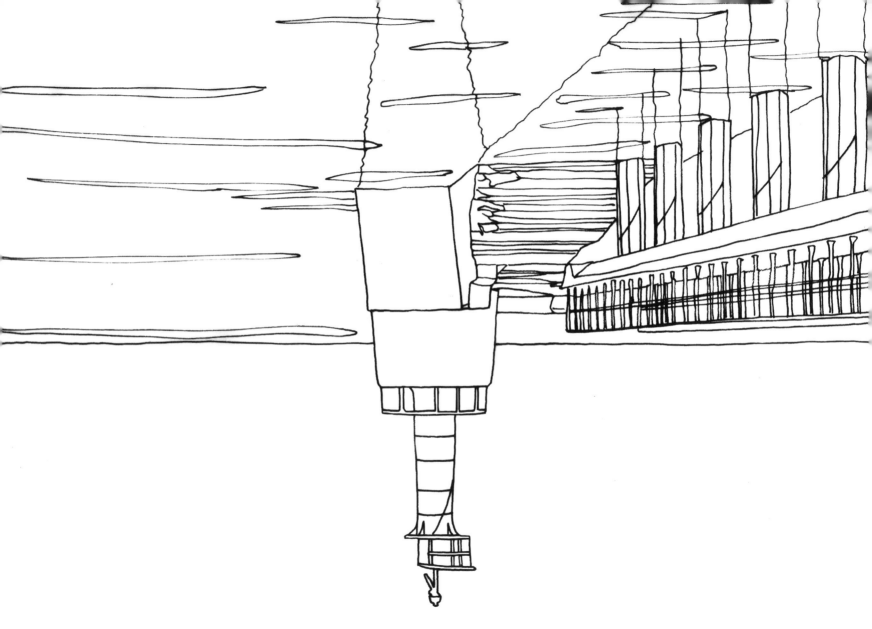

A view of Sycamore Gap in Hadrian's Wall ▸

Ruins of The Granary at
Housesteads Roman Fort, Hadrian's Wall ◀

◄ The Old Bridge, Haydon Bridge

Red Squirrels can be seen throughout northern
England, principally Northumberland, Cumbria,
Lancashire and the Yorkshire Dales ▶

Prudhoe Castle ▶

◀ Morpeth church

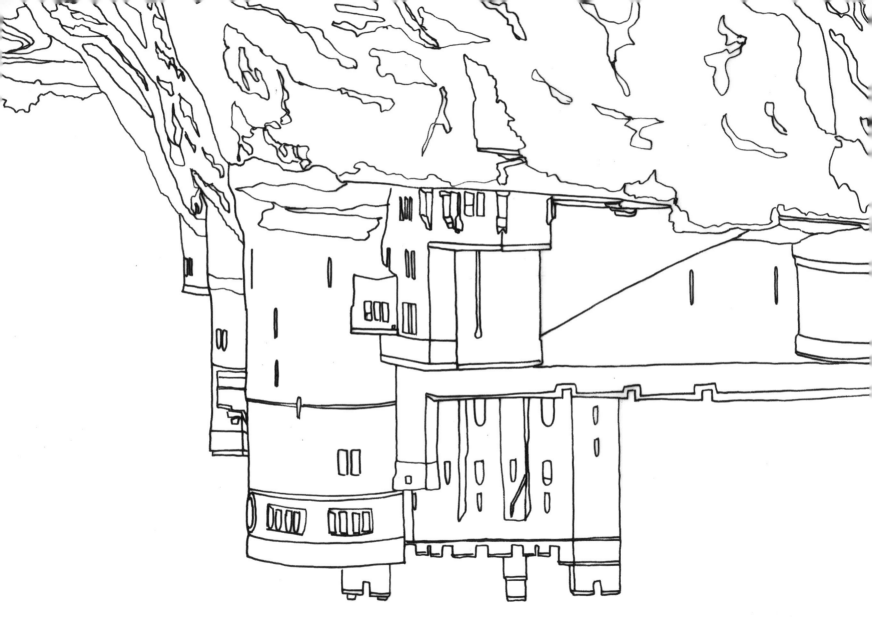

Bamburgh Castle ▸

Peacock at Kirkley Hall Zoological Gardens ▸

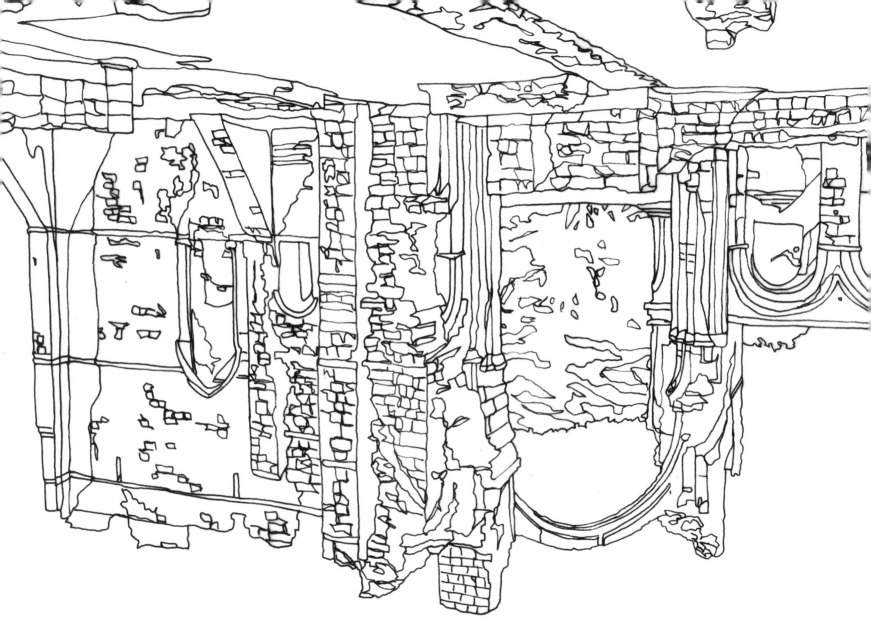

The ruins of Lindisfarne Priory on
Holy Island, founded *c.* 635 AD ▸

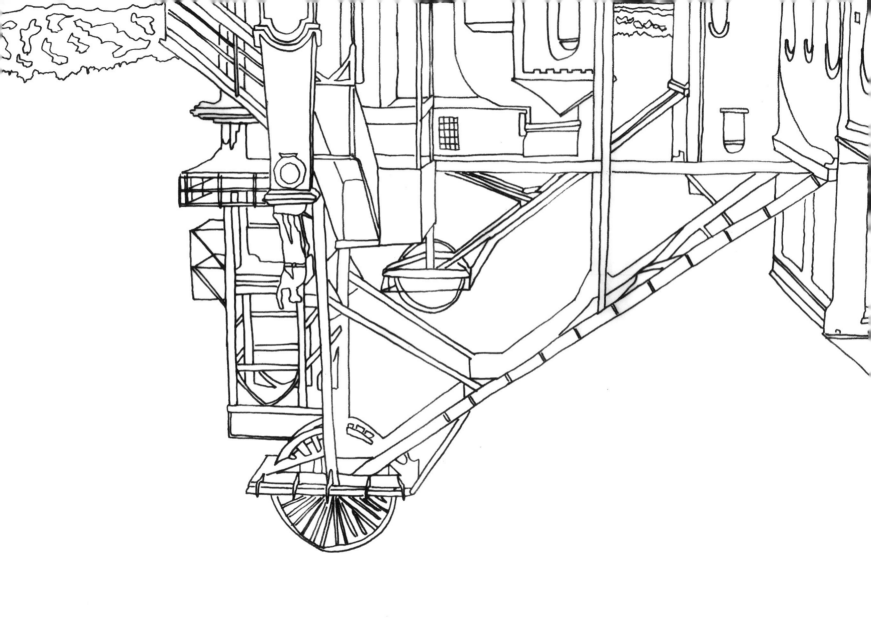

Woodhorn Northumberland Museum ▶

◀ View of the Upper Coquet Valley

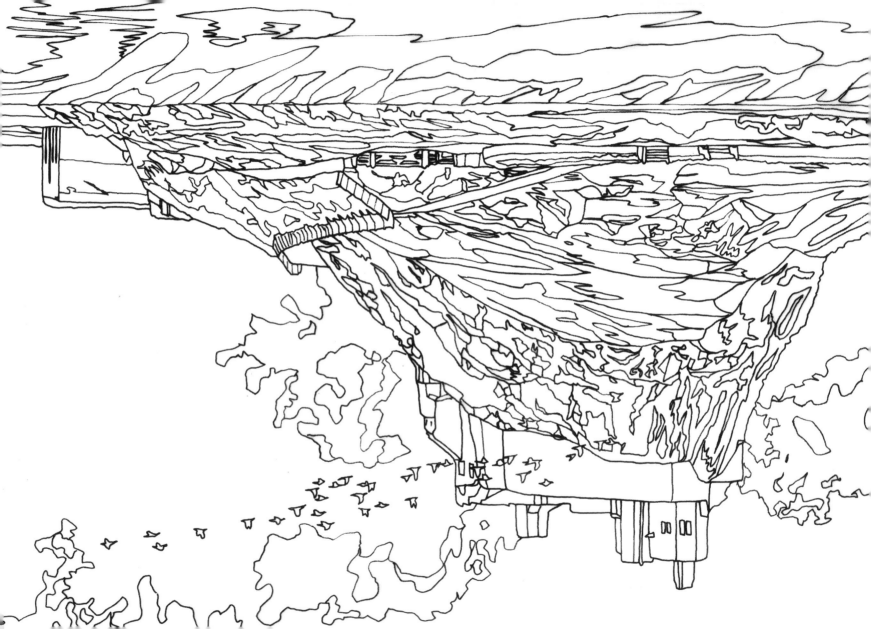

Lindisfarne Castle, Holy Island ◄

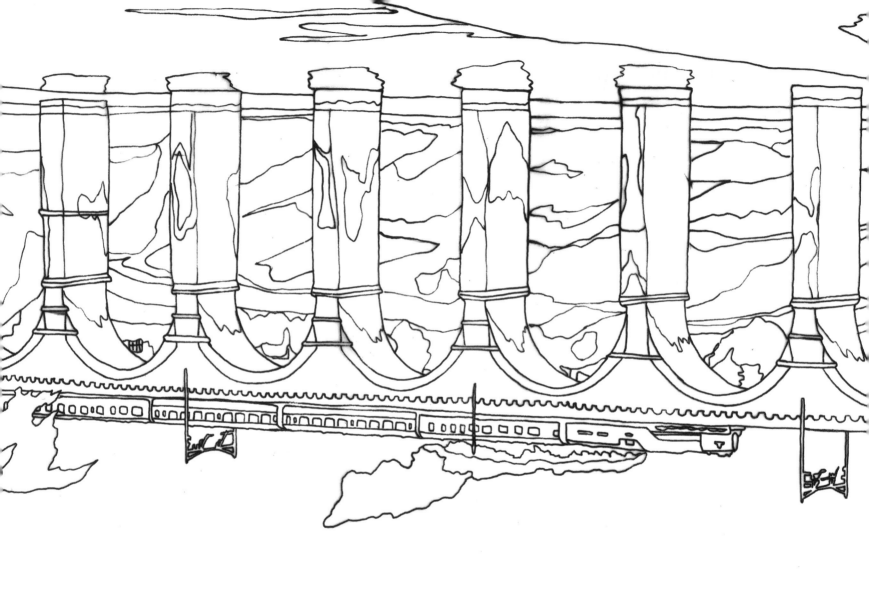

A Grade I listed railway viaduct, the Royal
Border Bridge spans the River Tweed between
Berwick-upon-Tweed and Tweedmouth ▸

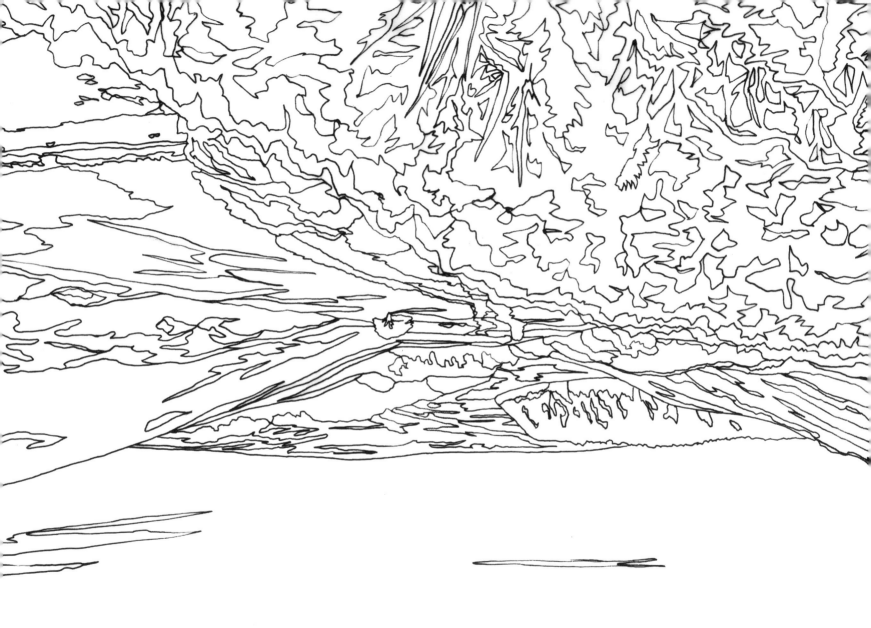

Bedlington station, c. 1950 ◄

Wallington Hall ▶

Aydon Castle ▶

Longstone Lighthouse, Farne Islands ▸

Blyth, *c.* 1950 ▸

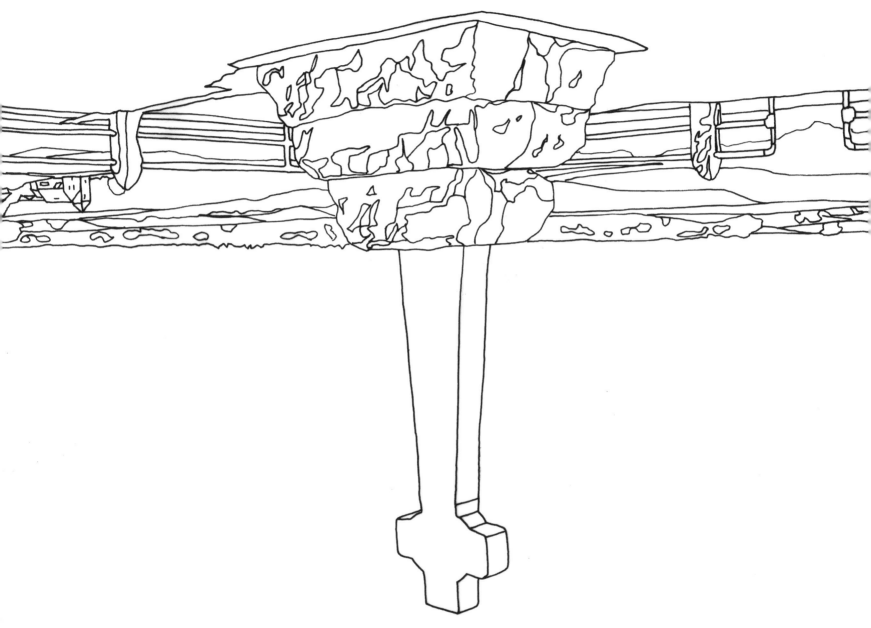

The Farne Islands are home to some of the
UK's most spectacular wildlife including puffins,
seals, and an incredible seabird population ▸

A young grey seal and cormorants on rocks at the Farne Islands ◄

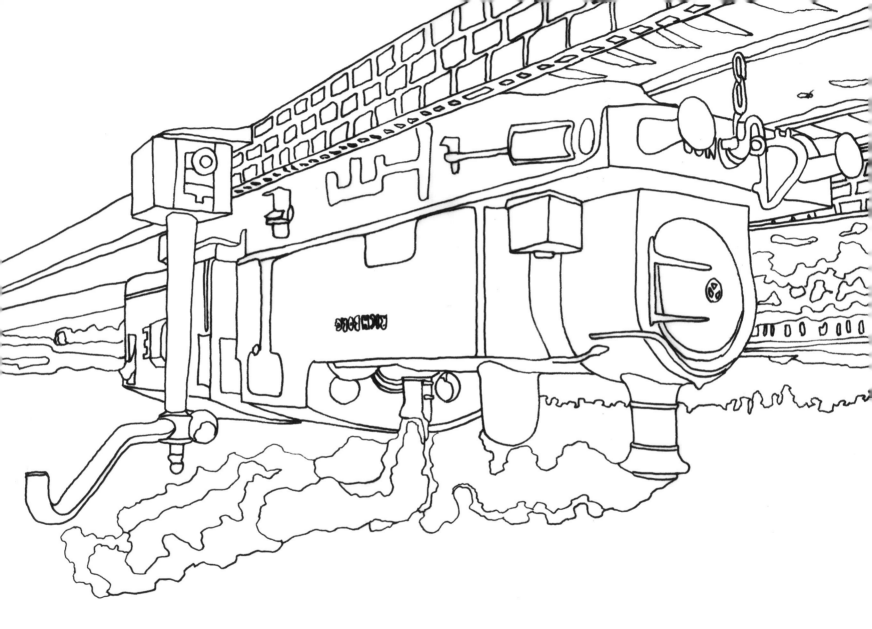

◀ Steam train at Aln Valley Railway

Built into a rocky hillside above a forest garden, Cragside was the country home of Lord Armstrong, and has been in the care of the National Trust since 1977 ▸

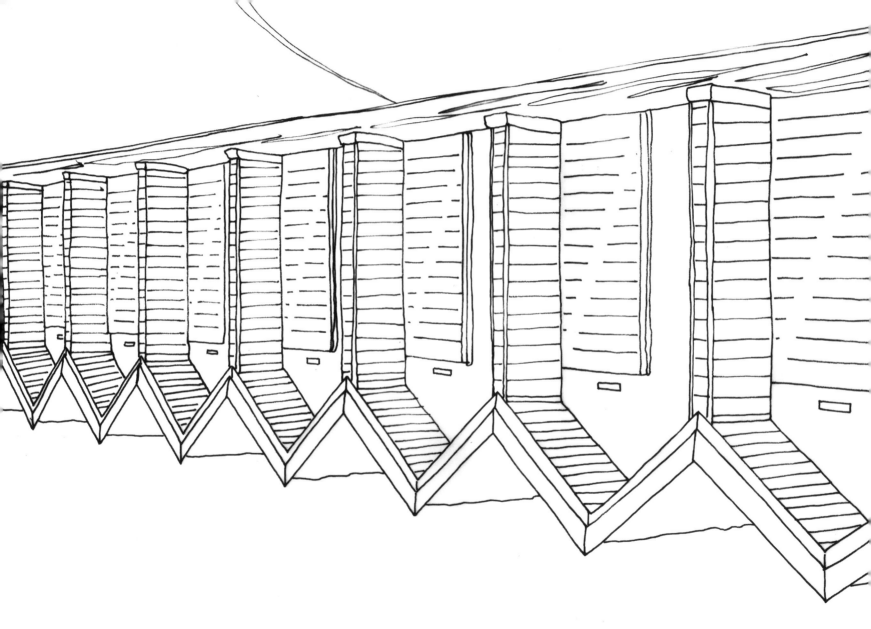

Cobles at Newbiggin-by-the-Sea, *c.* 1975 ▸

The Lord Crewe Arms at Blanchland ▶

Curlew at Lindisfarne National Nature Reserve ◀

The Town Hall, Berwick-upon-Tweed ▸

Alnmouth village ▶